Prayerserv

DONAL NEARY SJ

Prayerservices for Young People

the columba press

the columba press

84 Lakelands Avenue, Blackrock, Co Dublin, Ireland

First edition 1986
Cover by Bill Bolger
Typography by Liam Miller
Typeset and assembled by
Koinonia Ltd, Manchester
Printed in Ireland by
Mount Salus, Dublin

ISBN 0 948183 09 8

The publisher acknowledges the permission of the following to quote from their works: Darton, Longman & Todd and Doubleday & Co. for Jerusalem Bible quotations; Martin Brian & O'Keefe for quotations from Patrick Kavanagh; Wm Collins for a quotation from William Johnston SJ; the editor of *The Furrow* for a quotation from Peter Lemass. If we have used other copyright material in error we invite the copyright holder to communicate with us and we will put matters right.

CONTENTS

Introduction

Prayer Services for Young People is a series of Eucharistic and non-Eucharistic liturgies and services which are suitable for use in settings such as youth retreats, study-days, religious education and other occasions among the fifteen age group and upwards. The Masses in this volume are a companion to the author's *Masses with Young People* (Columba Press 1985).

The *reconciliation rites* are planned with retreats in mind. Their different themes suggest different aspects of reconciliation with God and with others. According to the type of group, leaders should use less of the material or add to it themselves. Some instruction about the sacrament of reconciliation may be necessary with young people. There is often a confusion about sin, about the forgiveness of God. The way of celebrating this sacrament is often a most impoverished human experience for young people. Care should be taken that the individual confession is not hurried, especially on a retreat. Thus the custom of waiting until all who wish to confess privately have done so before finishing the service is not recommended: it either drags out the service or hurries the individual conversation with a priest. Young people particularly like to be honest and frank. Encouragement should be given that they be open in their confession; a pastoral concern to make the sacrament accessible should not belittle the individual's desire to spend time talking over attitudes, values, behaviour and experience. On the other hand the possibility of an anonymous confession should also be a real choice; above all the priest should encourage them to confess in such a way that they have the consolation of having been open and honest with God. This is the wisdom of the church's concern with the *integrity* of the sacrament. That the sacraments are for the people is an ancient wisdom that has particular importance in the sacrament of reconciliation.

Well-known *christian symbols* are also presented for prayer. These are 'gateways to prayer' and involve both the daily experience and common wisdom of the community. These services, as the *Prayers Around Scripture* and *Prayers Around Concerns,* should be tailored both in timing and in content to suit the specific group.

Readers of parts of the services need to take time to prepare their piece.

Meditative and liturgical readings only lead to prayer when read with ease, ample pausing and meaning.

Music presents a certain problem since the variety of music used is quite large. Some suggestions are given from tapes easily available. Care should be taken that tapes are in good condition and are correctly selected before the service. Similarly the use of lighting and of candles is helpful for prayer, when a chapel or prayer-room is not available. Sensitive use of candles, lighting and music can transform a meeting-room with an atmosphere of prayer.

It is the author's hope that these liturgies and services will appeal to the hopes and desires of young people in such a way as to link the experience of their daily lives with the reality of God's presence and call in this experience, thus introducing them to a God who is close to them in Jesus Christ with the love that will be a strong basis and foundation for a life lived in his presence both in the years of youth and into later years.

Donal Neary SJ

1. Mass: Death of a Young Person

Introduction

Death is always a shock; even more so when it's the death of a young person, known to us for either a short or a long time. We have many words and few words: many words to say what's unimportant and few words to say the real, caring things we'd like to say to each other. We come here to remember a young person, to give thanks, even in our grief, for his/her life, to offer each other, and especially those who will most miss him, the consolation of our love and presence; and to offer also the promise of eternal life. Our consolations will be the joyful memories we have; our sadness is that a young person has gone from us, at an age we did not expect. Our sure hope is that the Lord our God will welcome him home, and that one day we will be united together in heaven. In the depth of our loss and hope we now pray and offer the sacrifice and thanksgiving of Jesus to his Father.

Penitential Rite

We come to God, knowing we need his mercy and forgiveness, and so in preparing to celebrate the Mass we call to mind our sins:
I confess. . .

Opening Prayer

Lord God, source of all life, in this world and the next,
we pray to you for our dear brother/sister. . .
Welcome him/her to the eternal joy of your kingdom
and give us all new hope in our sorrow
that one day we shall all be with you and with each other
in your home where every tear will be wiped away.
Grant this, we ask you, through Christ our Lord.

First Reading Is 55:6-11

A passage from Isaiah about the mystery of the ways of God, and how we cannot understand him always, nor understand why things happen as they do. But it is a confident statement of belief that nothing of what God makes or does is wasted, but is part of a loving plan.

A reading from the prophet Isaiah

Seek the Lord while he is still to be found,
call to him while he is still near.
Let the wicked man abandon his ways,
the evil man his thoughts.
Let him turn back to the Lord who will take pity on him,
for my thoughts are not your thoughts,
my ways not your ways – it is the Lord who speaks.
Yes, the heavens are high above the earth
as my ways are above your ways,
my thoughts are above your thoughts.

Yes, as the rain and the snow come down from the heavens and do not return without watering the earth, making it yield and giving growth to provide seed for the sower and bread for the eating, so the word that goes from my mouth does not return to me empty, without carrying out my will and succeeding in what it was sent to do.

This is the word of the Lord.

Responsorial Psalm Psalm 24

RESPONSE This day you will be with me in paradise.

1. Lord, make your ways known to me,
 teach me your paths.
 Set me in the way of your truth, and teach me,
 for you are the God who saves me. ℟.
2. All day long I hope in you
 because of your goodness, O Lord.
 Remember your kindness, Lord,
 your love, which you showed long ago.
 Do not remember the sins of my youth,
 but rather, with your love remember me. ℟.
3. Relieve the distress of my heart,
 free me from my sufferings,
 forgive all my sins. ℟.

Gospel Lk 24:1-8

We listen to the story of the resurrection of Jesus: this is the story which will give hope and consolation to us at the time of death. It is the reminder that everyone's life is for this world and the next. Our sure hope is that. . . who has died will share in this risen life of Jesus Christ.

A reading from the holy Gospel according to Luke.

On the first day of the week, at the first sign of dawn, they went to the tomb with the spices they had prepared. They found that the stone had been rolled away from the tomb, but on entering discovered that the body of the Lord Jesus was not there. As they stood there not knowing what to think two men in brilliant clothes suddenly appeared at their side. Terrified, the women lowered their eyes. But the two men said to them, 'Why look among the dead for someone who is alive? He is not here; he has risen. Remember what he told you when he was still in Galilee: that the Son of Man had to be handed over into the power of sinful men and be crucified, and rise again on the third day.' And they remembered his words.

This is the Gospel of the Lord.

Prayer of the Faithful

Let us pray now to God, the source of life; we pray for our friend who has died and also for those who mourn him/her; for ourselves and for all God's people.

1. Give eternal rest to. . ., and may the light of Jesus Christ shine upon him/her. Lord, hear us.

℟ Lord, graciously hear us.

2. Give to those who mourn him/her and will miss him/her the hope that he/she is with God, and let them always be thankful for the good of his/her life. Lord hear us. ℟.
3. We pray for all we know who have died, for family and friends; we pray especially for those who have died unmourned and unloved, Lord hear us. ℟.
4. We remember those who are widowed and all families who have lost a parent; may the Lord console them with his love, Lord hear us. ℟.
5. For those who have died in the cause of justice and of faith, we pray to the Lord. Lord hear us. ℟.

Grant to us, Lord God, a strong confidence
that you are Lord of the living,
and that nothing you have made is forgotten
in your sight and in your love.
We ask this through Christ our Lord.

Prayer over the Gifts
Lord God, Father of our Lord and Brother, Jesus Christ,
we give to you in bread and wine
the sadness at our loss and our thanks for . . .
May we all grow in hope this day
as we pray with him/her and all who have gone before us,
who have shared in the Bread of Life at your table.
We ask this in the name of Jesus the Lord.

Invitation to Communion
This is the body of the risen Lord, which we gratefully receive in memory of. . . and in our hope of eternal life. We are happy to be called to this Eucharist.

Communion Reflection
We can look on death in many ways:
a cloud that is dark,
a moment of intense aloneness,
a stinging fear;
an experience we resist and
don't wish to talk of.
We cannot avoid it nor escape it;
our experience this day
reminds us that death is a moment we all will face.
Can we see in it
the outstretched hand of God,
the light beyond the cloud that is dark;
or the companionship of Christ Jesus in this
fearful moment of aloneness?
As loved ones who have died in the peace of Christ
beckoned us into life,
they beckon us too,

our family and friends,
from beyond this earthly life
to share in the light and love
of the God whose death was the beginning
of the risen life on Easter morning.

Concluding Prayer

Lord God, your gift of the Body and Blood of Christ
is a sign of your unending love for your people.
May we be strengthened in our loss,
may we be encouraged in the darkness of death
and live our lives in service of you
as we hope to share in the risen life of Christ.
We make our prayer through Christ our Lord.

2. Mass for the End of School

Introduction

We're here today to remember, to pray and to think in hope about the future. We're at Mass to thank God for our times together, for the friends we made, for all we've learnt about life from teachers and from each other. We're here too so that we can pray for each other, each one's happiness in the future. This is a time of some sadness and some joy – sad to leave a lot behind, but joy in moving on. We pray also for ourselves in the coming exams, for peace of mind and for success in them. We look ahead in hope and know that God will be with us in the future as he has companioned us up to now. With a sense of joy and of thanks, we now begin our Mass.

Penitential Rite

We ask God's forgiveness for sin, for the ways, especially, we have been unkind to others and ways in which we have been neglectful of God, ungrateful to him or to others:
Lord, you have come to call sinners to yourself, Lord have mercy. ℟.
Lord, you forgave all who hurt you, Christ have mercy. ℟.
You plead for us at the right hand of the Father, Lord have mercy. ℟.

Opening Prayer

We thank you, Lord God, for the gifts of life and of love;
we thank you for the gifts of learning and of intelligence.
We ask you that you will always help us use these gifts in your service.
Give us a lively faith in you that will be stronger than any doubts we have,
a hope that will take us through any hard times of life,
and a love that is sincere as we give ourselves in your service.
We ask this through Christ our Lord.

First Reading 2 Thess 2:13–3:16

This reading is an encouragement from Paul to his people to be faithful to all they had learned from him, and to their faith. It is a prayer we might make for each other as we celebrate the end of our time together.

A reading from St Paul to the Thessalonians

But we feel we must be continually thanking God for you, brothers whom the Lord loves, because God chose you from the beginning to be saved by the sanctifying Spirit and by faith in the truth. Through the Good News that he brought he called you to this so that you should share the glory of our Lord Jesus Christ. Stand firm, then, brothers, and keep the traditions that we taught you. . . May our Lord Jesus Christ himself, and God our Father who has given us his love and such sure hope, comfort you and strengthen you in everything good that you do or say. Finally pray that the Lord's message may spread quickly and be received with honour as it was among you. . . But the Lord is faithful and he will give you strength and guard you from the evil one, and we have every confidence that you are doing and will go on doing all that we tell you. May the Lord turn your hearts towards the love of God and the fortitude of Christ. May the Lord of peace himself give you peace all the time and in every way. The Lord be with you all.

This is the word of the Lord.

Responsorial Psalm Psalm 27

RESPONSE The Lord is with us all the days of our life.

1. The Lord is my light and my shield
   whom shall I fear?
   The Lord is the stronghold of my life,
   against whom shall I be afraid? ℟.
2. I believe I shall see the Lord's goodness
   in the land of the living.
   Hope in him, hold firm and take heart,
   Hope in the Lord. ℟.

Gospel Lk 24:28-31

After a journey with his disciples Jesus breaks bread with them. This action of Christ, repeated in every Mass, is his promise and our certainty that he is with us always. We hear that promise today as we leave school.

A reading from the holy Gospel according to Luke

When they drew near to the village to which they were going, he made as if to go on; but they pressed him to stay with them. 'It is nearly evening' they said 'and the day is almost over.' So he went in to stay with them. Now while he was with them at table, he took the bread and said the blessing; then broke it and handed it to them. And their eyes were opened and they recognised him.

This is the Gospel of the Lord.

Prayer of the Faithful

We look now to the future and pray for everyone here, and for other intentions we remember.

RESPONSE Lord in your faithfulness, hear our prayer

1. Give good health, happiness and love in life to everyone here. Lord hear our prayer. ℟.
2. May everyone here find a job that gives satisfaction in their lives, may they find friendship and joy, and courage in times that are difficult. Lord hear our prayer. ℟.
3. Give us Lord, a sense of commitment in life; may we find our way of serving you in life, and use our talents for the good of others. Lord hear our prayer. ℟.
4. For anyone in our class who is sick, for those who are over-anxious about exams, for. . . who have died. We remember them and others who come to mind now. Lord hear our prayer. ℟.

Prayer over the Gifts

Lord God, may our prayer together
increase our faith in your companionship,
our hope in your love,
our love for your people.
As we offer this bread and wine,
may we be strengthened in our friendship with you,
now and forever.
We ask this through Jesus the Lord.

Communion Reflection

Our lives are marked forever
by those we meet;
the friendships we make and the love we experience,
the reconciliations and the quarrels,
the works we have tried to do together,
for each other and for those less fortunate.
All this has given us something that will last.

Long after we've forgotten the marks of our exams,
we'll remember the friendships, the times of growth,
the fun, the quarrels, the laughter, the jokes.
We'll remember how we helped each other grow as men and women,
in faith, in hope and in love.

May what we have done in this place
be given to many others in our lives.

Concluding Prayer

Lord, bless us as we go from this table of your love,
and from this place where you have been present among us.
Bless all those who have given their time to us,
bless all those who work here, teachers and staff.
May we go forth from here, confident in ourselves,
and willing to be your presence and help in our service of others.
We make this prayer through Christ our Lord.

3. Mass: Mary, Woman of Faith

Introduction

We see in Mary a woman of faith: she put her whole life on the line for God who asked her to be the mother of his Son. She is also a woman who made a very strong choice for God in her life, whose vocation, like ours, was to bring Christ to the world. She is the one who now lives with God as we one day hope to: fully alive in the love and in the life of eternity. Our Mass today is our remembrance of her and also our trust in her help, that she can help us by her prayers. We'll think in the Mass mainly of her faith and trust in God as she brought Jesus into the world. She was his first teacher; maybe in this Mass we can pray especially for our families.

Penitential Rite

As we begin our Mass we recall that we are sinful and selfish; that we need the forgiveness of God and of each other in our lives. We particularly ask his forgiveness for our neglect of our families and for any ways in which we unnecessarily cause them hurt, harm or pain. We ask pardon too for neglect of faith and of ways in which we have been arrogant and self-indulgent:

Lord Jesus, you are Son of God and Son of Mary, Lord have mercy. ℟.
Lord Jesus, you have come to save sinners, Christ have mercy. ℟.
Lord Jesus, you plead for us with our Father in heaven, Lord have mercy. ℟.

Opening Prayer

God our Father, we see in Mary, the mother of your Son,
a woman, like us in all but sin,
who welcomed your call in her life to be mother of your Son.
We ask that we be helped by her example and her prayers
to bring Jesus to birth again and again in our world
as we try to live lives in the spirit of his Gospel.
We ask this through Christ our Lord.

First Reading Is 9:1, 5-7

Because of the response of Mary to God, the light of God, Jesus Christ, entered into the world. This passage of the bible was one Mary would have read many times herself, as she pondered on her own calling by God – the promise of God to send Christ into the world.

A reading from the prophet Isaiah:

The people that walked in darkness
have seen a great light.
On those who live in a land of deep shadow
a light has shone.
You have made their gladness greater,
you have made their joy increase.
For there is a child born for us
a son given to us
and dominion is laid on his shoulders;
and this is the name they give him:
Wonder-Counsellor, Mighty-God,
Eternal-Father, Prince of Peace.
Wide is his dominion
in a peace that has no end.
From this time onwards and forever
the love of the Lord God will do this.

This is the word of the Lord.

Responsorial Psalm Psalm 99

RESPONSE The word was made flesh and lived among us.

1. Cry out with joy to the Lord all the earth,
   serve the Lord with gladness,
   Come before him, singing for joy. ℟.
2. Know that he the Lord is God,
   he made us, we belong to him,
   We are his people, the sheep of his flock. ℟.
3. Go within his gates giving thanks,
   enter his courts with songs of joy,
   give thanks to him and bless his name. ℟.

Gospel Jn 19:25-27

The faith and love of Mary for Jesus and his apostles are seen in her presence at the foot of the Cross. It shows her as a woman of courage, who didn't try to escape the hard experiences of life and of love. She was there when she was needed; she followed through to the end her choice to love and serve God.

A reading from the holy Gospel according to St John

Near the cross of Jesus stood his mother and his mother's sister, Mary the wife of Clopas, and Mary of Magdala. Seeing his mother and the disciple he loved standing near her, Jesus said to his mother, 'Woman, this is your son.' Then to the disciple Jesus said, 'This is your mother.' And from that moment the disciple made a place for her in his home.

This is the Gospel of the Lord.

Prayer of the Faithful

Let us make our prayers to God, remembering people we want to pray for, especially our families.

RESPONSE Lord, be gracious and bless us.

1. We pray for our parents, brothers and sisters, for all in our families who may be in trouble or sickness, that the Lord may be close to them and bless them. ℟.
2. We pray for families who are in trouble through lack of employment or decent housing, for families in whom there are conflicts and poor relationships, that they may be helped by others who see their needs. ℟.
3. For any of our family who have died, that the Lord may welcome them home and comfort those who miss them. ℟.
4. We pray that we may follow Mary's example, growing strong in faith and in love, asking for the courage to follow God's call in our lives. ℟.

We pray now through Mary's intercession
that we may be helped in our lives by her prayer and example;
may we be people of faith, hope and love,
and may we be always strengthened in our lives
by the promise of everlasting love and joy in heaven.
We make this prayer through Christ our Lord.

Prayer over the Gifts

Lord, accept our gifts of bread and wine,
signs of our faith in you,
small signs of our thanks to you.
We ask you that you change us to be more like your Son,
as we receive his body and blood,
the gift of Mary's son,
Jesus Christ, in whose name we pray.

Invitation to Communion

This is the lamb of God, Jesus Christ, Son of God and Son of Mary.
We are happy to be called to this Eucharist.

Communion Reflection

The coming of Christ

Nobody thought he'd come like he did:
born like a poor child, in a borrowed house,
the son of a woman seeming no different from any other,
except in her glowing faith and huge generosity.
Long after the kings who envied him have been forgotten,
the name of Jesus, Son of God and Son of Mary,
is remembered in lands not even then heard of.
Long after Mary's own birthplace is forgotten,
or the shape of her face and the age of her death,
we remember that she was a woman who gave to God
her whole life, her whole womanhood,
and because of that 'all generations call her blessed'.

Mary, you remind us of what's best in our human nature –
sympathy, compassion, motherhood, love and care.
You remind us too that we are made not just for this life
because as you are now, we one day shall be
through the grace and gift of God.

Concluding Prayer

Give health of mind and body to us, Lord God,
through the prayers and love of your Son's mother.
Give us too a faith like hers,
a confidence in you like hers
and a hope like hers.
We make this prayer through Christ Our Lord.

4. Healing Service

This service begins with some suitable music, during which candles are lit in the form of a cross, either in the middle of the group on the floor or on a table, or on the altar. A quiet mood suits best a healing service and the music and lighting, if possible, should reflect this. After the music the gospel story is read.

Gospel Mk 3:1-5

This is a story of healing in the ministry of Jesus. The man with the withered hand could be any of us. We all have weaknesses in ourselves that need strengthening: resentments can give way to tolerance, guilt to sorrow and forgiveness, grudges to understanding. Like the man in this story we too need 'to stand out in the middle' and face the darkness and weakness in ourselves and ask the Lord for this peace and healing.

A reading from the holy Gospel according to St Mark

Jesus went into a synagogue and there was a man there who had a withered hand. They were watching to see if he would cure him on the sabbath day. . . He said to the man with the withered hand, 'Stand up out in the middle!' Then he said to the man, 'Stretch out your hand.' He stretched it out and his hand was better.

This is the Gospel of the Lord.

Homily

The homily from the priest or leader of the group should refer to our need for healing. . . we all carry the wounds of our sins and the sins of others with us. . . grudges, resentments, angers, despair which weigh us down in God's presence and with others. . . we have been hurt and the memories of others' words need to be healed. . . we suffer a lot of guilt over sin. . . how we treat others in how we talk of them, use them for our own purposes in matters of sexuality, of wealth, of influence. . . God's healing power helps us see ourselves and others whole, allowing his love to forgive the sins, heal the wounds and the hurts of our lives. We need his healing. . . the type of healing love that only God can give, even though we need also to forgive each other. . . we need also to face our hurts and our need of healing. . . like the man in the Gospel standing out in the middle. . . and then be open and humble enough to allow the forgiveness and healing of God in Christ to reach us.

Reflection

We carry around with us
the scars of our past.
What others have said and how they have failed us
still pains and hurts and we're intolerant.
What we've done ourselves is in our memory
a cause of shame and guilt and mistrust of ourselves.
We carry scars and they'll be always there;
let's bring them to Christ and to each other,
be touched with his healing power and love
so that the scars, while still part of ourselves,
no longer pain
but are reminders of his forgiveness
and his love.

Pause here for silent reflection and prayer, with some suitable music in the background.

Responsorial Psalm Psalm 27

RESPONSE In you, O Lord I put my trust.

1. The Lord is my light and my help,
   whom shall I fear?
   The Lord is the stronghold of my life,
   before whom shall I shrink? ℟.
2. It is your face, O Lord, that I seek;
   hide not your face.
   Dismiss not your servant in anger;
   you have been my help. ℟.
3. Do not abandon or forsake me,
   O God my help!
   Though father and mother forsake me,
   The Lord will receive me. ℟.

At this point individuals may come forward from the group and ask for healing. If appropriate, the leader and whole group pray for each person, holding hands outstretched to the person, some of them imposing hands on each person's head, saying together:

May the Lord Jesus forgive you your sins,
heal the wounds of your sins
and bring you to life everlasting.

Intercessions

RESPONSE Hear our prayer.

1. Give each of us, Lord, the openness and courage to forgive anyone who has been a cause of hurt. Lord in your mercy ℞.
2. May we each be healers of others in our ability to listen and to be sympathetic. Lord in your mercy ℞.
3. We pray for people whose lives have been made difficult by the dishonesty and the hurt of others. Bless them with the grace of reconciliation. Lord in your mercy ℞.
4. For families who are estranged and for any of our friends who have fallen out with each other. Lord in your mercy ℞.

Lord make us instruments of your peace,
where there is hatred, let us sow love,
where there is injury, pardon,
where there is doubt, faith,
where there is darkness, light,
where there is despair, hope.
Give us hearts of compassion and of love,
attitudes to others which are tolerant and understanding,
and in this way may we be your presence among your people.

Gospel Jn 21:1-14

The resurrection of Jesus is a moment of reconciliation and of healing; it is a time when he forgave the disciples their denials and neglect of him. It is a time too when the disciples forgave each other for their lack of faith, and their lack of support of each other. When there is forgiveness and healing among people, then the resurrection happens again for God's people. With that in mind, we hear one of the resurrection stories where Jesus meets his disciples again, gives them signs of his new life and love in inviting them to a meal on the seashore.

A reading from the holy Gospel according to St John

Later on, Jesus showed himself again to the disciples. It was by the Sea of Tiberias, and it happened like this: Simon Peter, Thomas called the Twin,

Nathanael from Cana in Galilee, the sons of Zebedee and two more of his disciples were together. Simon Peter said, 'I'm going fishing.' They replied, 'We'll come with you.' They went out and got into the boat but caught nothing that night.

It was light by now and there stood Jesus on the shore, though the disciples did not realise that it was Jesus. Jesus called out, 'Have you caught anything, friends?' And when they answered, 'No,' he said, 'Throw the net out to starboard and you'll find something.' So they dropped the net, and there were so many fish that they could not haul it in. The disciple Jesus loved said to Peter, 'It is the Lord.' At these words 'It is the Lord,' Simon Peter, who had practically nothing on, wrapped his cloak around him and jumped into the water. The other disciples came on in the boat, towing the net and the fish, they were only about a hundred yards from land.

As soon as they came ashore they saw that there was some bread there, and a charcoal fire with fish cooking on it. Jesus said, 'Bring some of the fish you have just caught.' Simon Peter went aboard and dragged the net to the shore, full of big fish, one hundred and fifty-three of them; and in spite of there being so many the net was not broken. Jesus said to them, 'Come and have breakfast.' None of the disciples was bold enough to ask, 'Who are you?'; they knew quite well it was the Lord. Jesus then stepped forward, took the bread and gave it to them, and the same with the fish. This was the third time that Jesus showed himself to the disciples after rising from the dead.

This is the Gospel of the Lord.

Concluding Prayer

We thank you, Lord, for this gift of healing.
We thank you that we can come to you in our need
and know, in our prayer and life with each other,
that we can renew the past of sin and guilt
with your life of forgiveness and hope.

At the end of the service, priests should be available for the Sacrament of Penance.

5. Reconciliation with Each Other

The service may start with music and there should be a psalm between the readings. During confession and reconciliation time, there might be some hymns or taped music. The confession time should not be too long: it can in fact continue after the service, so there is no need to wait until all confessions are finished before beginning the last part of the service.

The service should end with a joyful hymn, followed by some taped music so that as many of the group may stay on in the chapel or place of prayer for as long as they like within an atmosphere of prayer.

Introduction
We come from many different backgrounds; sometimes our backgrounds unite us, other times divide us. We're divided into college and non-college, worker and unemployed, young and old, wealthy and poor; some are popular, others feel inadequate; we have different levels of faith and of love of God. Our past experience of hurt and of happiness, of failure and success, of home and of love, partly make us what we are. The sacrament of penance is a sacrament of reconciliation; not only of forgiveness, but of healing of divisions. Our relationship with God is affected by our relationships with each other; our way of relating to each other brings us closer to Christ or away from him. This prayer of reconciliation is an invitation from God to see beyond our differences to what unites us; to put our own successes and failures, hurts and happiness into the perspective of his love for us. One of the Gospel's strongest calls is: be reconciled with one another.

First Reading 2 Cor 5:17–6:1

We know that Christ has reconciled us to himself and to God. He has healed divisions among us; we need to continue that healing. Let's hear this scripture as an invitation to reconciliation among each other.

A reading from the second letter of St Paul to the Corinthians

For anyone who is in Christ, there is a new creation; the old creation has gone, and now the new one is here. It is all God's work. It was God who reconciled us to himself through Christ and gave us the work of handing on this reconciliation. In other words, God in Christ was reconciling the world to himself, not holding men's faults against them, and he has entrusted to us the news that they are reconciled. So we are ambassadors for Christ; it is as though God were appealing through us, and the appeal that we make in Christ's name is: be reconciled to God. For our sake God made the sinless one into sin, so that in him we might become the goodness of God. As his fellow workers, we beg you once again not to neglect the grace of God that you have received.

This is the word of the Lord.

Psalm Psalm 51

RESPONSE Have mercy on me God in your kindness.

1. Have mercy on me, O God, in your goodness,
   in your great tenderness wipe away my faults;
   wash me clean of my guilt,
   purify me from my sin. ℟.
2. For I am well aware of my faults,
   I have my sin constantly in mind,
   having sinned against none other than you,
   having done what you regard as wrong. ℟.
3. Be my saviour again, renew my joy,
   keep my spirit steady and willing;
   and I shall teach transgressors the way to you,
   and to you the sinners will return. ℟.

Gospel Lk 23:33-34

The forgiveness of Jesus from the Cross is the example of reconciliation he gives. He offers forgiveness and reconciliation to his 'enemies.' That too is what we can do; we can be people who invite others to be reconciled with us as we try to give over to God the grudges and resentments and fears that keep us apart.

A reading from the holy Gospel according to Luke

When they reached the place called The Skull, they crucified him there and the two criminals also, one on the right, the other on the left. Jesus said, 'Father, forgive them; they do not know what they are doing.' They then cast lots to share out his clothing.

This is the Gospel of the Lord.

Meditation on Reconciliation
As a candle is lit, one of the group prays
Lord Jesus, be our light.
Be the light of forgiveness and of healing,
be the light of goodness in each person.
Help each of us to see the light of God,
given by you in your life, death and resurrection,
in everyone here.
Be our light, Amen.

As another candle is lit
Holy Spirit burn away the selfishness within us,
enlighten us, each of us here,
so that we can see the resentments and the grudges,
the bitterness and the hollowness in our lives.
Enlighten us, that we can see our selves,
our goodness and our sin;
encourage us in your warmth
that we can allow the selfishness be burned away
in the light and the joy of your love for us.
Be the light of our lives. Amen.

Examination of Conscience
In silence now let's think of how we have failed the Lord Jesus in our relations with each other:

thinking harshly and judging without evidence
talking of another's weaknesses and ignoring the good
using another in any way, emotionally, for our own success, sexually
looking down on another for reasons of wealth or family, school or job
and in any other way. We are now sorry. We confess to God. . .

I confess. . .

A time for private confession may follow.
During the time of confession, there is opportunity also to offer people a sign of peace, a word of encouragement, and, if necessary, a word of reconciliation.

After confessions, a bowl of water is carried into the centre of the group and one of the group says:

I am the living water; if anyone comes to me and drinks, they will not be thirsty again.

Father, you have cleansed us of sin and division;
you have invited us to a new life of freedom
when we scatter divisions among us
and see each other as children of God,
brothers and sisters.
May this water be a reminder of our baptism, when you made us your children;
may it unite us in the love which flows all our lives from you
and may it spread and sprinkle this love among us.
Let us hear you say now, as you say to us in Jesus,
you are my beloved, my son, my daughter,
and in our hopes and our love, our reconciliation and forgiveness
may we also hear your word to listen to him,
Jesus, our Lord, now in this life and into eternity.

6. Reconciliation with God

Introduction

As candles are lit around the altar and the chapel or room where the rite is to be held, a hymn is sung or some music played on tape.
A reader begins:
The sacrament we're celebrating now is the celebration of God's forgiveness. We all need this; we know that the less-good side of ourselves, or the mean side of ourselves and the sinful side of ourselves can each be operative in how we relate to God and each other. We carry with us a lot of guilt for what we do and say; our prayer now is to bring this to God, and hear his words of forgiveness spoken to each of us. We find it hard to forgive ourselves, and so we pray that this forgiveness of God, seen in Christ, will heal the guilt we may feel and that we'll feel truly sorry.

Opening Prayer

We pray, Lord God, that we may know ourselves and open ourselves honestly to you. We ask you for the courage to face what's evil in ourselves and the honesty to accept the gift of your forgiveness. Be with us, Lord, as we pray; be with us in the Spirit of reconciliation, and in the forgiveness of Jesus, your Son, who has died and is risen from death for our sins. We ask this in the name of Jesus the Lord.

Scripture Readings

Someone once compared sin to a river which has burst its banks: a river flows easily, gently, watering the land around it. In its banks it's in the right place and is ordered, beautiful. If it bursts its banks, it's disordered and spoils crops, floods fields, destroys houses. Something has gone wrong. Sin is like that – the beauty and order of our relationships with God and each other have gone wrong. Or it can be like another picture: a bird trying to fly but held to the ground by a single but tough thread. It can't do what it's meant to do. No longer free, it's confined in a life less free than it could have. Sin and selfishness keep us from loving God and each other in a way that gives human happiness. God knows this and forgives us, he knows this yet calls us into the freedom of his forgiveness. He is the one who in Jesus' death and resurrection takes away our sins. Let's listen now to some of his words about forgiveness.

First Reading

A reading from the prophet Isaiah

Do not be afraid, you will not be put to shame,
do not be dismayed, you will not be disgraced;
for you will forget the shame of your youth.
For now your creator will be your husband,
he is called Lord of the whole earth.
Like a forsaken wife, distressed in spirit,
the Lord calls you back.
I did forsake you for a brief moment,
but with great love I will take you back.
With everlasting love I have taken pity on you.
For the mountains may depart,
the hills be shaken,
but my love for you will never leave you,
and my covenant of peace will never be shaken, says the Lord.

This is the word of the Lord.

At this point a candle might be given to each person, and lit individually from the principle candle. During this some music can be sung or played. The music should be meditative, quiet. Or a few verses of a psalm might be spoken, e.g. Psalm 103.

Gospel

Jn 8:1-11

Still holding candles, we listen to the Gospel story of Jesus' forgiveness of a woman.

A reading from the holy Gospel according to John

At daybreak he appeared in the Temple again; and as all the people came to him, he sat down and began to teach them.

The scribes and Pharisees brought a woman along who had been caught committing adultery; and making her stand there in full view of everybody, they said to Jesus, 'Master, this woman was caught in the very act of committing adultery, and Moses has ordered us in the Law to condemn women like this to death by stoning. What have you to say?' They asked him this as a test, looking for something to use against him. But Jesus bent down and started writing on the ground with his finger. As they persisted with their question, he looked up and said, 'If there is one of you who has not sinned, let him be the first to throw a stone at her.' Then he bent down and wrote on the ground again. When they heard this they went away one by one, beginning with the eldest, until Jesus was left alone with the woman, who remained standing there. He looked up and said, 'Woman, where are they? Has no one condemned you?' 'No one, sir' she replied. 'Neither do I condemn you,' said Jesus 'go away, and don't sin any more.'

This is the Gospel of the Lord.

Reflection and Confession

The priest may now lead a short meditation.

Imagine yourself now in a place you like. . . maybe by the sea, or in the hills, or at a river. . . or in a park. . . somewhere you can be alone. . . picture that for a while. . . the different things in the place, the air on your face, the sounds you can hear. . . relax there. . . be at peace. . . in the presence of God. . . and of Christ. . . let him be with you in that place. . . sitting down beside you. . . tell him what is between you and him and God in your life. . . anything you really want to say sorry to him for. . . hear him saying 'I do not condemn you'. . . be as honest as you can. . . what's mean in your life. . . the people you hurt even if you don't mean to. . . people you might use, get mad at when it's just a selfish thing to do. . . hear him saying 'I do not condemn you'. . . then rest for a while there with him. . . relax in the friendship and forgiveness of Christ. . . *(music)*.

During a pause for prayer and reflection, private confession is available. Those who would like confession later may do so at the end of the service.

Final Scripture and Prayer

In the joy of being forgiven we now hear God's word about christian community – a call to love and forgiveness of others.

Reading Col 3:12-15

A reading from the letter of St Paul to the Colossians

You are God's chosen race, his saints; he loves you, and you should be clothed in sincere compassion, in kindness and humility, gentleness and patience. Bear with one another; forgive each other as soon as a quarrel begins. The Lord has forgiven you; now you must do the same. Over all these clothes, to keep them together and complete them, put on love. And may the peace of Christ reign in your hearts, because it is for this that you were called together as parts of one body. Always be thankful.

This is the word of the Lord.

Meditation

What's the forgiveness of God like?
Maybe like water washing over a rock,
gradually wearing away the blemishes,
smoothing, cleaning, glistening,
but not erasing what was past.
God's forgiveness gives a new look to a person;
the past is always there but not a blemish.
Or it's like the healing of a scar,
the wound remains but no longer pains.
The wound on the skin or the mark on a rock,
reminders of other times which have been
with the help of God and his love
transformed so that they are part of a person
but not the whole person.
We have a prayer for all of us
that we can see ourselves as God does,
men and women cleansed and healed in forgiveness;
and let that be the power and grace
that will help us forgive ourselves.
Let our sins and faults with all our generosity
become stepping stones on which we can dance to God.

Final Prayer

We receive from this moment and prayer, Lord,
the grace of your forgiveness and we accept this with thanks.
May the forgiveness of your love
which reaches into our depths
be the forgiveness which flows from us
to others who need forgiveness from us.
We make this prayer through Christ our Lord.

7. You are my Friends

Begin this service with some suitable music, maybe a Taizé chant, or a song about friendship. Any song about the faithfulness of God, for example, *Be Not Afraid,* would also be suitable. During the music one or more of the group places a symbol of friendship in a prominent place, along with a symbol of the friendship of Christ, like a cross or a candle.

Introduction

When Jesus wanted a description of his relationship with us, he used the word, *friend.* He calls his apostles friends, because, he says, 'I have made known to you everything I have learnt from my Father.' His friendship with them, and with us, is a deep sharing of everything that is important to him, and a giving of himself that leads even to death. To help us appreciate the friendship of Christ, let's first think of our human friends:

Guided Reflection

In your own memory now, with your eyes closed, think of a friend. . . picture him or her. . . what the friend looks like. . . tone of voice. . . the way he/she says your name. . . the tone in which you say his/her name. . . remember good times together. . . when you shared your life. . . your problems. . . your hopes. . . any bad times and reconciliations?. . . note something you like in this friend. .. thank God for this. . . thank God for your friend. . . if you see that you need to repair this friendship in any way, ask God's help. . . again thank him for this friend.

Meditation

We are moulded and remoulded by those who have loved us
and though that love may pass,
we remain, nonetheless, their work. . .
No love, no friendship can ever cross the path of our destiny
without leaving some mark on it forever.

Francois Mauriac

Readings

We change attitudes and our personality grows in relationships with others; the people who are our friends shape us and influence us. The same can happen in our relationship with Christ. In this piece of his letter to the church in Philippi, St Paul explains how he has changed because of Jesus' friendship with him:

First Reading Phil 3:5-8

A reading from the letter of St Paul to the Philippians

I was born of the race of Israel and of the tribe of Benjamin, a Hebrew born of Hebrew parents.

As for the Law, I was a Pharisee; as for working for religion, I was a persecutor of the Church; as far as the Law can make you perfect, I was faultless. But because of Christ, I have come to consider all these advantages that I had as disadvantages. Not only that, but I believe nothing can happen that will outweigh the supreme advantage of knowing Christ Jesus my Lord. For him I have accepted the loss of everything, and I look on everything as so much rubbish if only I can have Christ and be given a place in him.

This is the Gospel of the Lord.

Gospel Lk 5:1-11

The apostles too found their lives changing because of the friendship of Jesus. They received the friendship of Jesus, as Peter in this story, and knowing his love found themselves called by him, even when they did not feel worthy themselves. Jesus' friendship asks us to look on ourselves as accepted, forgiven and called by God.

A reading from the holy Gospel according to Luke

Now he was standing one day by the Lake of Gennesaret, with the crowd pressing round him listening to the word of God, when he caught sight of two boats close to the bank. The fishermen had gone out of them and were washing their nets. He got into one of the boats – it was Simon's – and asked him to put out a little from the shore. Then he sat down and taught the crowds from the boat.

When he had finished speaking he said to Simon, 'Put out into deep water and pay out your nets for a catch.' 'Master,' Simon replied 'we worked hard all night long and caught nothing, but if you say so, I will pay out the nets.' And when they had done this they netted such a huge number of fish that their nets began to tear, so they signalled to their companions in other boats to come and help them; when these came, they filled the two boats to sinking point.

When Simon Peter saw this he fell at the knees of Jesus saying, 'Leave me, Lord; I am a sinful man.' For he and all his companions were completely overcome by the catch they had made; so also were James and John, sons of Zebedee, who were Simon's partners. But Jesus said to Simon, 'Do not be afraid; from now on it is men you will catch.' Then, bringing their boats back to land, they left everything and followed him.

This is the Gospel of the Lord.

In silence now for a while, or with some music playing softly in the background, allow the words of God to sink in; hear him saying to you 'You are my friend'. . . as it was true for the apostles, it is true for you.

Prayer for Others

We ask you, Lord, to bless and give your love to all we think of now. . . for friends who have been good and helpful in our lives. . .

We pray for those who have no friends. . . for young people who find it hard to know that they are loved by you. . .

We pray for those who are lonely, who are depressed by their isolation. . . and pray that each of us can be sensitive to everyone's need for both your love, O Lord, and the love of friends. . .

Be with us Lord
in all we say and do in our friendships;
make us ready to forgive and to understand,
to forget ourselves and our own concerns
and look on the concerns of others as equally important.
Help us always, Lord, to know you as a friend,
and in knowing this to offer our friendship to others.
This we ask of God our Father
through Jesus our Lord.

8. Come, Follow Me

Begin with music suitable for prayer and then read the Gospel passage:

First Gospel Reading Mt 9:9

The story of Jesus calling one of his apostles. Matthew would have known of Christ and probably watched him from afar, attracted by him and feeling that he would like to commit his life to this man. It's a simple story, just giving the essential words of Jesus. Let them speak to you.

A reading from the holy Gospel according to Matthew

As Jesus was walking on from there he saw a man named Matthew sitting by the customs house, and he said to him 'Follow me.' And he got up and followed him.

This is the Gospel of the Lord.

Second Gospel Reading Lk 5:1-11

Answering the call of Christ is not as simple as that. In other stories the process of choosing to do so is spelt out more fully. Peter's call was to follow the Lord, but he needed many reminders of it. He was told to 'cast out into the deep a second time' and he felt great unworthiness in responding to the call of Jesus. Hear the words of the Lord addressed to you:

A reading from the holy Gospel according to Luke

Now he was standing one day by the Lake of Gennesaret, with the crowd pressing around him listening to the word of God, when he caught sight of two boats close to the bank. The fishermen had gone out of them and were washing their nets. He got into one of the boats – it was Simon's – and asked him to put out a little from the shore. Then he sat down and taught the crowds from the boat.

When he had finished speaking he said to Simon, 'Put out into deep water and pay out your nets for a catch.' 'Master,' Simon replied 'we worked hard all night long and caught nothing, but if you say so, I will pay out the nets.' And when they had done this they netted such a huge number of fish that their nets began to tear, so they signalled to their companions in the other boat to come and help them; when these came, they filled the two boats to sinking point.

When Simon Peter saw this he fell at the knees of Jesus saying, 'Leave me, Lord; I am a sinful man.' For he and all his companions were completely overcome by the catch they had made; so also were James and John, sons of Zebedee, who were Simon's partners. But Jesus said to Simon, 'Do not be afraid; from now on it is men you will catch.' Then, bringing their boats back to land, they left everything and followed him.

This is the Gospel of the Lord.

Reflection
Reflect for a few moments now on your own talents. . . how you think you might serve the Lord. . . in the friendships you can offer. . . in the work you might do for him. . . the hungry you might feed. . . the lonely you can befriend. . . the sick you could heal. . . or any other way you might do the Lord's work. . . or how?. . . as a husband or wife. . . a priest. . . a religious. . . how you might feel the Lord is calling you to be a partner with him in spreading the message of his Gospel. . . offer yourself to him. . . in thanks for what you have given me, Lord. . . I return to you in your service. . . end with the words 'Come, follow me' echoing in your heart and mind.

Reflection
Lord,
The film I just saw was about the miseries and injustices of the world;
The headlines in the newspapers report violence, murder, death;
And I think of other particular suffering around us:
 thousands of children sick in India,
 death and loneliness in Belfast,
 drug-addicts exploited by pushers,
 kids hooked on glue,
 ignorance through lack of education,
 sickness through lack of medical care,
death on the streets.

Lord, how can I respond to the cries of your people?

I think of the less-known sufferings:
The anxieties and depressions of lonely men and women;
Of those who attempt suicide;
Of those who drown their cares in over-indulgence in alcohol.

What can I do to help?
I want to, Lord,
I want my life to be a channel of your love to them:
But what can one man, one woman, do?

Help me, Lord, to believe that I can help,
And give me the courage and generosity to offer myself in service,
That my life might be like a candle,
Giving light to others.

The Calm Beneath the Storm.

Prayer for Others

We pray for people who are following Christ in different situations, for parents and families, that they can together create places of love and of forgiveness in our world. . .
For your people in many parts of the world who are suffering imprisonment or harrassment for their dedication to the faith and justice of God's call. . .
That young people have the openness to hear the call of God in their decisions about their life's plans, and may answer courageously what the Lord is asking of them. . .
That all God's people may know that they are a people called to be partners with him in creating a world of peace and of justice. . .

A time for private and shared prayer

A Blessing

May you bless us all, Lord God,
with the gentle reminders of your presence and call;
may we hear you as the one whose call
offers a life based on the joy of giving ourselves in love to others,
and may we be generous in offering our lives to you,
as you have offered yours to us.
We pray in the name of Jesus the Lord.

9. What You do for Others, You do for Me

The service begins with some music; *Ubi Caritas (Laudate)* would be suitable. During the music a candle may be lit and a cross placed in the centre of the group or some prominent position.

Introduction
The word of God links intimately our relationship with God and the way we treat others. A few verses of the prophet Amos sums it up:
This is what the Lord asks of you,
only this:
to act justly,
love tenderly,
and walk humbly with your God.

The Lord himself says:
Whatever you do for my people on earth, you do for me;
and he also says:
Not those who say Lord, Lord, will enter the kingdom of heaven,
but those who do the will of my Father.

This makes our faith really down-to-earth; it's the type of faith we want – not one that is 'pie in the sky' but one connected with the bits and pieces of everyday.

Gospel Lk 10:29-37

Jesus tells one of the world's best stories when he wants to make this point about treating others well. He speaks of a man who is mugged on a roadside and passers-by are afraid to help. The story speaks to all our fears of getting involved in being just to others, especially when it's risky. It's always risky to help others; we may lose something of ourselves in the process. Jesus could tell this story honestly and convincingly because he was describing himself; the one who acted towards others like the good Samaritan.

A reading from the holy Gospel according to Luke

The man was anxious to justify himself and said to Jesus, 'And who is my neighbour?' Jesus replied, 'A man was once on his way down from Jerusalem to Jericho and fell into the hands of brigands; they took all he had, beat him and then made off, leaving him half dead. Now a priest happened to be travelling down the same road, but when he saw the man, he passed by on the other side. In the same way a Levite who came to the place saw him, and passed on the other side. But a Samaritan traveller who came upon him was moved with compassion when he saw him. He went up and bandaged his wounds, pouring oil and wine on them. He then lifted him on to his own mount, carried him to the inn and looked after him. Next day, he took out two denarii and handed them to the innkeeper. 'Look after him,' he said 'and on my way back I will make good any extra expense you have.' Which of these three, do you think, proved himself a neighbour to the man who fell into the brigands' hands?' 'The one who took pity on him' he replied. Jesus said to him, 'Go, and do the same yourself.'

This is the Gospel of the Lord.

Intercessions

Lord in your mercy hear our prayers for those whose lives are made difficult by the way others treat them:

RESPONSE Lord, in your mercy hear our prayer.

1. We pray for people who are mistreated in the poverty of their housing, in the poor allocation of jobs, in the inequality of education. Lord, hear us. ℟.
2. We pray for men and women, young and old, who are mistreated and exploited by others, especially people exploited sexually; may they be healed by the companionship and love of others. Lord, hear us. ℟.
3. For men and women who are oppressed because of the colour of their skin or for their faith, in all parts of the world. Lord, hear us. ℟.

Pause now for shared petitions on this or other topics.

Reflection and Prayer

The way God looks on injustice is well expressed by the Irish poet Patrick Kavanagh:

Do you hear that noise, Mother,
That comes over the sea?
Is that God the Father raging
In His Eternity?

That is only war, darling,
Drunk men returning
From the pubs of their pleasure,
They'll be sober by morning.

Do you hear that whisper, Mother,
That follows the sigh
From the house of Injustice?
What was that going by?

That was God raging, child,
Something to fright
More than the shouting
Of a whole drunken night.

('War and Peace' from *Collected Poems*)

Reflection

Justice is the way we treat each other;
in the daily, warm-cold conversations of families and friends;
justice is when we see each man and woman, child and old person,
as a brother and sister in Christ
and so respect and enjoy them like that.
Justice sees a person whole and entire,
not just as a nice body, a fat bank-balance
or in any other way that uses them.
Justice is to see people as Jesus did:
children of his Father.

It's also the way we demand for everyone
a life free of oppression and poverty,
a place to live, the right to schooling,
the freedom to live in equal opportunity
without prejudice of skin or of creed.
Justice is to form with Jesus Christ
the type of society he dreams of,
a society of love and justice,
of peace, truth, holiness and reconciliation.
We pray now to be part of that building –
that we can be partners with God in our world:

Help us, Lord, we ask,
to be people
who act justly,
love tenderly
and walk humbly with you.
Help us to be men and women
like your Son Jesus
who gives his life for the
good of his people,
for we are all brothers and sisters in him.

The service ends with a sign of peace and then with some music as people might like to pray silently for a while.

10. Vocation in Life

Introduction

Vocation is a call to partnership with God in the work of creating the world, of redeeming and renewing his people and of being an instrument to spread his Gospel wherever we are. It is a call to discipleship – to follow Jesus Christ in the way he related to men and women, and in the way he related to society. It is a disturbance of our own personal peace and complacency, for the Gospel of Christ will always challenge us to new ways of loving God's people. Vocation may be to marriage, priesthood, religious life, single life. It is a call to pray, to serve, and to share christian life with others. We pray now for light to know God's invitation in our lives and for courage to follow a call to be partners with him in our world.

The call of Christ to a person is sometimes clear and very attractive; other times unclear. The cost is always high and the resistances of human weakness are equally clear. We go through ups and downs in decision-making, and in the process we begin to know what God wants of us and what we want ourselves. You and God work in partnership in your life's vocation. Some reflections help us meditate on this:

In decision I am alone;
even though the decision is for a way of life
that many share,
still, it is my decision.
It flows from the unique, warm-cold world that is mine,
and although touched by the encouragement and questioning
of many others,
it is my decision, mine only.
I stand alone,
ears straining to hear the music that is for my marching feet.
Only I will march in my step,
in unique step with the One who calls *my name*.
Although I am chosen,
I choose personally to say 'Yes,'
hearing the voice 'Come'
through the feelings, convictions and desires that are mine.
A serene, challenging 'Come'
which reaches year by year, wave-like on the shell-shore of my heart,

refreshing old hopes with new joy,
painfully reaching into the sands of selfishness
to tear away what clings on, unwanted.
Shining through love's meaning and love's joys,
all the time saying 'Come.'
Calling firmly and faithfully,
promising neither comfort nor cosiness
but faithful, trustful companionship.

A poem by Patrick Kavanagh expresses the experience of being touched by something of God, and following where it may lead, even though the 'touching' may not ever again be as intense:

Upon a bank I sat, a child made seer
Of one small primrose flowering in my mind.
Better than wealth it is, said I, to find
One small page of Truth's manuscript made clear.
I looked at Christ transfigured without fear –
The light was very beautiful and kind,
And where the Holy Ghost in flame had signed
I read it through the lenses of a tear.
And then my sight grew dim, I could not see
The primrose that had lighted me to Heaven,
And there was but the shadow of a tree
Ghostly among the stars. The years that pass
Like tired soldiers nevermore have given
Moments to see wonders in the grass.

('Primrose,' from *Collected Poems*)

Following a vocation is a call to trust – to trust in God and to trust in yourself:

Go places, this new day, where your heart would.
Walk where you will and in the walking know
The way is yours.
Allow for storms.
At the end of the day they'll prove
That your heart was wise and your choice was good.

M. Rider

Allow some time for personal meditation either silently with music in the background (e.g. *Ubi Caritas – Laudate*) or with a *guided reflection:*

Guided Reflection

Recall a time when you felt drawn by some way of life. . . marriage. . . priesthood. . . religious life. . . or any way of life or job in life which would involve you in service to others. . . mull over the question for a while. . . how do you feel about following this 'nudge' within. . . or not following. . . hear the words of scripture 'Come, follow me' and respond to the Lord as you want to. . . in thanks for your life vocation. . . in petition for clarity. . . in hope that you will know what he wants. . . asking him for courage or for light or whatever comes to your mind and heart now.

After some silence listen to one of the calls of the Gospel:

Gospel Mk 10:17-22

A reading from the holy Gospel according to Mark

He was setting out on a journey when a man ran up, knelt before him and put this question to him, 'Good master, what must I do to inherit eternal life?' Jesus said to him, 'Why do you call me good? No one is good but God alone. You know the commandments: You must not kill; You must not commit adultery; You must not steal; You must not bear false witness; You must not defraud; Honour your father and mother.' And he said to him, 'Master, I have kept all these from my earliest days.' Jesus looked steadily at him and loved him, and he said, 'There is one thing you lack. Go and sell everything you own and give the money to the poor, and you will have treasure in heaven; then come, follow me.' But his face fell at these words and he went away sad, for he was a man of great wealth.

This is the Gospel of the Lord.

Depending on the size and context of the group, they might share reflections after that meditation and Gospel. The leader might also encourage them to talk to someone about the question of their vocation in life if they think that might be helpful.

Final Prayer

Lord God, help each person here to know and find your will;
help us to be trustful of you and of ourselves
to follow our desires to live our life in your service.
May we always be men and women who centre our lives on you,
hearing joyfully your call to be your companion,
and knowing your faithfulness in all our lives.
We make this prayer through Christ our Lord.

11. Who is Jesus Christ?

In the centre of the group place either a cross, or an ikon of Christ, or some other symbol of Christ. If suitable you might expose the Blessed Sacrament. A song might be played at the beginning, such as *Dwelling Place* (from the album of that name by St Louis Jesuits) or a chant such as *Jesus, Remember Me* (Taizé music).

Introduction

Our prayer now is about the person of Jesus Christ. The One who is the centre and core of our christian faith is the one who says of himself:
I am the Way, the Truth and the Life.
I am the Resurrection.
I have come that they may have life.
I call you friends because I have made known to you all I have learnt from my Father.

After some time of silent prayer, the leader prays:
Lord Jesus, you are mystery to us,
you are Son of Mary and Eternal Son of God.
You call us friends.
One who comforts our troubles
and disturbs our peace;
One who companions us every step
of life's journey,
the One who gives joy,
the One who brings life,
the One who promises resurrection,
the One who is friend at all times.
Help us know you,
and knowing you, believe you,
and believing in you, live in your friendship,
which is the love of Father, Son and Spirit.

The group at this point might like to share some of their experiences of their relationship with Christ. If it is suitable and in context they could share some response to the question: how do you see Jesus in your life? Can you name a time when you experienced the joy and comfort of his companionship, and a time when you found his companionship disturbing?

Gospel Mk 1:29-39

The following passage from Mark's gospel gives some typical pictures of Jesus: compassion and care for people, prayer with his Father, and the call to his followers to go and work with him:

A reading from the holy Gospel according to Mark

On leaving the synagogue, he went with James and John to the house of Simon and Andrew. Now Simon's mother-in-law had gone straight to bed with fever, and they told him about her straightaway. He went to her, took her by the hand and helped her up. And the fever left her and she began to wait on them.

That evening, after sunset, they brought to him all who were sick and those who were possessed by devils. The whole town came crowding round the door, and he cured many who were suffering from diseases of one kind or another; he also cast out many devils, but he would not allow them to speak, because they knew who he was.

In the morning, long before dawn, he got up and left the house, and went off to a lonely place and prayed there. Simon and his companions set out in search of him, and when they found him they said, 'Everybody is looking for you.' He answered, 'Let us go elsewhere, to the neighbouring country towns, so that I can preach there too, because that is why I came.' And he went all through Galilee, preaching in their synagogues and casting out devils.

This is the Gospel of the Lord.

Meditations

Do not think that to enter the mystery of Christ
is to escape from the world.
Again I say that the mystery of Christ
is centred on his cross.
This means that it is the mystery
of the poor, the sick,
the afflicted, the deranged,
the imprisoned, the dying
and all those suffering people with whom Jesus identifies.
It is the mystery of the exploited, the manipulated,
the terrorised, the oppressed.

It is the mystery of nuclear war, of hunger,
of injustice, of human anguish.
It is the mystery
of you and me
when we suffer
and when we sin.
Christian mystical experience,
far from flying from the suffering and sinful world,
is an entrance to its very heart.

William Johnston SJ, *The Wounded Stag*

But above the words of Jesus
comes the example of his life.
Born in a stable;
no influence to get room in the inn. . .
a citizen of Nazareth,
a bad address,
the kind of place you wouldn't mention
if looking for work.
An exile, like a million or so Chileans
who can't live in their native country
for the same reason as Jesus.
A manual worker,
his hands frequently dirty,
often cut,
a renegade preacher, 'on the run.'
Finally abandoned by his friends and supporters
he is alone at the mercy of soldiers –
you don't have to be long in Latin America to know what that might mean.
He gets the death of a criminal slave,
naked on the cross. . .

Peter Lemass, *The Call to be Poor*

I welcome you, Lord, into my life;
into the love and work of my days and nights,
into the hopes and fears that are mine;
I welcome you thankfully
because you are a friend,

because you accept me, as you accept us all,
and because you are forgiving.

Lord help me to learn from you;
to learn that God is friend and father,
to learn that I am worth his love and worth your death;
help me to learn from you how to love,
how to live in your love,
accepting and forgiving others in turn.

This, Lord, is my prayer,
to be like you and not lose myself in the process:
to be the person you have made me
and to grow into the man or woman you are shaping;
help me to live for you, to work with you,
and to share your Gospel of peace and love
with the unique personality that is mine.

Thank you, Lord, for your friendship,
thank you for what I learn from you;
thank you that at this moment I can call you
Friend, Teacher, Lord and God.

The time of prayer can end now with some music, giving people time and space to pray for whatever length of time they wish.

12. Trust

Introduction

The strength of a relationship depends on the level of trust we have with another person: trust that we can share a secret or a problem; trust that we are accepted as the person we are. Trust is the soil of friendship's growth. The relationship we have with God is like that with a best friend. He is one whom we can be open with, let into the secret parts of our life, know we are fully accepted and forgiven. We can trust that what he asks of us is good too; the challenge of his call will bring out the best in us. We pray for a while now, thanking him for those we can trust, asking that others can trust us and that we can grow in trust with him.

Guided Reflection

Think for a few moments of a person you can trust. . . maybe a friend, a family-member. . . a teacher. . . a trusted adult. . . remember that person. . . picturing him or her. . . remember times when you felt you could trust him/her. . . notice your feelings. . . thanks. . . hope. . . trust. . . turn now to God as you know him and thank him for that person.

Gospel Mt 14:22-33

A story of trust in the Gospel is when Jesus asked Peter to walk towards him on the water. This is a call to trust God's presence in the big moments of life, both joyful and sorrowful. We remember the story not because Peter 'began to sink' but because he found he could trust in Jesus.

A reading from the holy Gospel according to Matthew

Directly after this he made the disciples get into the boat and go on ahead to the other side while he would send the crowds away. After sending the crowds away he went up into the hills by himself to pray. When evening came, he was there alone, while the boat, by now far out on the lake, was battling with a heavy sea, for there was a head-wind. In the fourth watch of the night he went towards them, walking on the lake, and when the disciples saw him walking on the lake they were terrified. 'It is a ghost,' they said, and cried out in fear. But at once Jesus called out to them, saying, 'Courage! It is I! Do not be afraid.' It was Peter who answered. 'Lord,' he said, 'if it is you, tell me to come to you across the water.' 'Come,' said Jesus. Then Peter got out of the boat and started walking towards Jesus across the water, but as soon as he felt the force of the wind, he took fright and began to sink. 'Lord! Save me!' he cried. Jesus put out his hand at once and held him. 'Man of little faith,' he said, 'why did you doubt?' And as they got into the boat the wind dropped. The men in the boat bowed down before him and said, 'Truly, you are the Son of God.'

This is the Gospel of the Lord

Prayer for Others

RESPONSE Lord may we grow in trust of you and of each other.

1. Bless all those whom we have trusted and who have helped us in times when we needed another to trust. ℟.
2. May each of us be people who can be trusted, who can listen to others and not condemn them. ℟.
3. For young people who feel isolated and alone; we pray that they will find others whom they can trust. ℟.
4. For our parents, that trust between them and us may grow; for our teachers and others who guide us; may they be blessed in their lives. ℟.

Lord God, make us people who can trust and be trusted;
help us to know in your love for us that we are your children
and that your friendship with us
can be the foundation of our trust in each other.
Give us always, in youth and all the years of our life,
a trust in your companionship
so that one day we may live forever in your love.
We ask this through Christ our Lord.

Reflections

Trust me to love even when the pain is fierce
Or in the nothing of the darkest night:
Take love into the shadows where self-hatred lurks
and trust that you were worth the death of God.

Michael Hare-Duke

If you try me
send me out
into the foggy night
so that I cannot see my way.

Even if I stumble,
this I beg, that I
may look and smile serenely,
bearing witness
that you are with me
and I walk in peace.

Helder Camara

Final Prayer
Be with us, Lord, we pray
source of life, generosity and trust,
consolation in times that are good,
comfort in times that are troublesome,
companion always.
This prayer we make in the name of Jesus the Lord.

13. Justice

Opening Prayer

Lord Jesus, we see your face in the hunger
and homelessness of your people.
We hear your cry in their loneliness.
Their tears of injustice are your tears.
We see your hands nailed on the cross
of intolerance and of bigotry and of violence,
and your side pierced with a lance of hatred and of harshness
where people cannot worship as they wish,
celebrate your presence as they wish,
speak your Gospel as they wish.
We ask you, Lord Jesus,
to open our eyes and our ears
to ways in which people hurt each other;
we ask too that we be people
who are your justice and your compassion,
your love and your friendship in our world.

Guided Reflection

In your own stillness picture someone who is poor. . . someone who is homeless, hungry. . . someone who is suffering through the injustice of others. . . or through the system of society in which we live. . . a traveller, a man seeking a job and who can't find one. . . someone of your own experience or a picture you've seen. . . look at him/her for a moment, feel for the person. . . with that person's face in your mind, hear the words of Jesus – 'what you do for the least of my people, you do for me.' Stay with that face, and with those words for a while. . . then do the same with another, and another, as you feel moved. . . pray for each of these people. . . just look at them and pray. . . don't make any plans or feel any guilt. . . pray, look, look and pray.

Gospel Lk 7:18-23

The signs of the kingdom are the signs that Jesus spoke about to John the Baptist. Let these words of Jesus enthuse you and challenge you to be his hands, his voice, his ears, his heart in the world.

A reading from the holy Gospel according to Luke

The disciples of John gave him all this news, and John, summoning two of his disciples, sent them to the Lord to ask, 'Are you the one who is to come, or must we wait for someone else?' When the men reached Jesus they said, 'John the Baptist has sent us to you, to ask, "Are you the one who is to come or have we to wait for someone else?"' It was just then that he cured many people of diseases and afflictions and of evil spirits, and gave the gift of sight to many who were blind. Then he gave the messengers their answer, 'Go back and tell John what you have seen and heard: the blind see again, the lame walk, lepers are cleansed, and the deaf hear, the dead are raised to life, the Good News is proclaimed to the poor and happy is the man who does not lose faith in me.'

This is the Gospel of the Lord.

Final Prayer

May all we say and do to others, Lord God,
begin and end with you.
May we be people of peace in your world,
people of justice and of compassion.
May we be people like you,
and we pray now as always to God our Father
in your name.

14. Christian Unity

(suitable particularly for an inter-church group)

Prayer

Lord Jesus Christ, you prayed earnestly for the unity of your followers; we pray for this too and ask forgiveness and healing of divisions. We pray for those who suffer pain through christian disunity and ask you that we may see you as the unity and centre of our faith. We ask this of your Father in your name.

First Reading 2 Cor 5:17-20

A reading from the second letter of St Paul to the Corinthians

For anyone who is in Christ, there is a new creation; the old creation has gone, and now the new one is here. It is all God's work. It was God who reconciled us to himself through Christ and gave us the work of handing on this reconciliation. In other words, God in Christ was reconciling the world to himself, not holding men's faults against them, and he has entrusted to us the news that they are reconciled. So we are ambassadors for Christ; it is as though God were appealing through us, and the appeal that we make in Christ's name is: be reconciled to God.

This is the word of the Lord.

Gospel Jn 18:1-11

Jesus does not repay violence with violence.

A reading from the holy Gospel according to John

After he had said all this Jesus left with his disciples and crossed the Kedron valley. There was a garden there, and he went into it with his disciples. Judas the traitor knew the place well, since Jesus had often met his disciples there, and he brought the cohort to this place together with a detachment of guards sent by the chief priests and the Pharisees, all with lanterns and torches and weapons. Knowing everything that was going to happen to him, Jesus then came forward and said, 'Who are you looking for?' They answered, 'Jesus the Nazarene.' He said, 'I am he.' Now Judas the traitor was standing among them. When Jesus said, 'I am he,' they moved back and fell to the ground. He asked them a second time, 'Who are you looking for?' They said, 'Jesus the Nazarene.' 'I have told you that I am he' replied Jesus. 'If I am the one you are looking for, let these others go.' This was to fulfil the words he had spoken, 'Not one of those you gave me have I lost.'

Simon Peter, who carried a sword, drew it and wounded the high priest's servant, cutting off his right ear. The servant's name was Malchus. Jesus said to Peter, 'Put your sword back in its scabbard; am I not to drink the cup that the Father has given me?'

This is the Gospel of the Lord.

Cross of Nails

A number of nails scattered in the form of a cross might be used as a symbol of unity, of suffering and of the cruelty of disunity. These can be placed in a place where everyone can see them, e.g. in the middle of the group. Candles in the form of a cross may also be a suitable symbol if the size of the group prevents a symbol of nails being adequately visible.

Confession

RESPONSE Lord have mercy.
For disunity of intolerance and of harsh judgment in our lives, Lord have mercy. ℟.
For disunity of bitterness and despair between people, Lord have mercy. ℟.
For disunity of war and violence in the name of religion, Lord have mercy. ℟.
God, healer and Reconciler in Jesus Christ,
be with us now, your chosen ones.
Touch our hearts and the hearts of all your people
with the reconciling power of love.
Let us know the pain of disunity among your people,
let us feel the urgency of working for unity
and let us give thanks today
for your work of unity and reconciliation
among your people.
This we ask through Christ our Lord.

15. Dreams

We admire people who dream big; who look at their lives and the world around them and dream of how they could live in such a way as brings some more hope, justice, peace and love to that world. We dream of peace in a war-torn country, of employment in a people suffering lack of jobs, of good health and plenty where there is sickness and starvation. Each of us has dreams of our future – involving our job, our state of life, the love we will give and receive, the type of parents we might be, the husband or wife we'll marry, the way we'll serve God. Our dreams are our hopes. God plants good dreams within us: we can call them good desires. Desires of wanting to do good things in our lives. We'll pray about that now.

Gospel Mk 10:17-22

This is about a young man who wanted to follow the best desires in his heart. Jesus' way of life attracted him to follow him. Watch the way Jesus encourages him – talks to him about his dreams, loves him and gives him a free invitation to follow that dream. Something blocks the young man from making a way of life out of his dreams, and his desire for eternal life.

A reading from the holy Gospel according to Mark

He was setting out on a journey when a man ran up, knelt before him and put this question to him, 'Good master, what must I do to inherit eternal life?' Jesus said to him, 'Why do you call me good? No one is good but God alone. You know the commandments: You must not kill; You must not commit adultery; You must not steal; You must not bring false witness; You must not defraud; Honour your father and mother.' And he said to him, 'Master, I have kept all these from my earliest days.' Jesus looked steadily at him and loved him, and he said, 'There is one thing you lack. Go and sell everything you own and give the money to the poor, and you will have treasure in heaven; then come, follow me.' But his face fell at these words and he went away sad, for he was a man of great wealth.

This is the Gospel of the Lord.

After the Gospel the group could discuss the story briefly, if this is suitable. Maybe they could try to imagine a finishing to that story with some of these questions:

Why do you think the young man found it hard to follow his dream?
What was Jesus' reaction when he went away?
Do you think Jesus would try again?
Do you think the young man would return again to Christ?

Meditation
Become quiet. . . listen for a few moments to the sounds around you. . . become still in yourself. . . think over the various 'dreams' you have for your life. . . what you would like to do and be. . . recall what the important things for you in life are. . . love. . . job. . . friendship. . . serving others. . . as you think over your future allow some words of Jesus to reach you. . . he loved the young man. . . he loves you. . . 'you will have treasure in heaven'. . . 'follow me'. . . think for a while how this affects the dreams of your life and your future. . .

16. Prayer around the Cross

Begin with some music or a hymn. Any music or hymn suggestive of the passion of Christ is suitable, such as *Jesus, Remember Me* (Taizé music) or *O Sacred Head* (Bach's Chorale).

During the singing or playing of music, a cross should be placed either in the centre of the group or some prominent position. This can be a picture like an ikon, or a tasteful crucifix, or a cross of nails or of wood made by the group.

Scripture

We listen to some phrases of scripture, both old and new testaments, which recall the mystery of the cross in the life of Jesus and in the life of his people:

Read slowly, with pauses between phrases, reciting or singing the response:

℟. Dying you destroyed our death.
Rising you restored our life.
Lord Jesus come in glory.

Ours were the sufferings he bore,
ours the sorrows he carried. ℟.

Harshly dealt with, he bore it humbly,
he never opened his mouth,
like a lamb that is led to the slaughter-house,
like a sheep that is dumb before its shearers,
never opening its mouth. ℟.

Today you will be with me in paradise. ℟.

Father, forgive them, for they do not know what they are doing. ℟.

His soul's anguish over
he shall see the light and be content. ℟.

Was it not ordained that the Christ should suffer
and so enter into his glory? ℟.

Meditation

Become aware of some way in which you suffer yourself. . . in body. . . in spirit. . . maybe aspects of your personality which bring hardship to you. . . become aware of whatever is the cross in your own life. . . an illness. . . a handicap. . . a facet of your personality like a relationship that makes you suffer. . . bitterness. . . anger. . . sexuality. . . in all that, see the cross of Jesus as a sign of love. . . forgiveness. . . hope. . . bring your cross to his. . . he carries it for you. . . allow yourself be hopeful because of his words to you. . . I love you.

Prayer

We ask you, Lord Jesus, that your cross be a sure hope for each of us.
May we see your love and companionship as healing our hurts
giving us new confidence and trust in you and in ourselves.
As the cross is a sure sign of risen glory,
may we see the crosses of our lives as invitations
to resurrection, trust and hope in your power.

The service may end here; part 2 may continue now if you have time, or at another time.

A child once made a picture of the crucifixion, but left out the figure of Christ. Asked why, the child finished the picture: where the head of Christ would have been was a poster with the words *to be continued*. We pray now about the mystery of the passion of Christ continuing in the passion of his people.

Scripture Meditation

I was hungry and you never gave me food; I was thirsty and you never gave me anything to drink; I was a stranger and you never made me welcome, naked and you never clothed me, sick and in prison and you never visited me. Then they will ask: 'Lord, when did we see you hungry or thirsty, a stranger or naked, sick or in prison, and did not come to your help?' Then he will answer, 'I tell you solemnly, in so far as you neglected to do this to one of the least of these, you neglected to do it to me.'

Meditation

Writing of the horror of the concentration camps, Elie Wiesel described his own feelings when he saw a child being hanged:

On that day
horrible even among those days of horror,
when the child watched the hanging (yes!) of another child,
who, he tells us, had the face of a sad angel,
he heard someone behind him groan:
'Where is God?
Where is he?
Where can he be now?'
and a voice within me answered:
'Where?
He is here;
He has been hanged here,
on these gallows.'

Intercessions

A time may follow for intercessions for people whose lives are made miserable and who are oppressed through the exploitation and injustice of others. Members of the group can make these prayers out beforehand, or they may be spontaneous.

The service continues with veneration of the cross, either kissing or touching it and then making the sign of the cross. The service can end with a prayer or be open so that people may finish their prayer at their own time.

Final Prayer

Lord Jesus we pray in the mystery of your cross.
In life and in death,
in joy and in sorrow,
in oppression and in our fears,
hold your cross before us
so that we see you, the Lord of death and of suffering,
of joy and resurrection, now and forever.

17. Prayer with a Candle

This service of prayer focusses on a christian symbol, and uses the symbol as a 'gateway to prayer'. It is a way of linking the word of God in Jesus Christ with some of the strong images Jesus used to talk about himself.

A candle should be placed in a central place within the group, either as part of a circle, or in the centre of a circle, or at the top of a room where everyone can see it. More candles can be placed around the chapel or room when that is suitable.

As the candle is being lit, the following Scripture is read *slowly:*

I am the light of the world
anyone who follows me will not be walking in the dark
but will have the light of life.

In your light
we see light.

Anyone who claims to be in the light
but hates his brother
is still in the dark.
But anyone who loves his brother is living in the light
and need not be afraid of stumbling;
unlike the man who hates his brother and is in the darkness,
not knowing where he is going,
because it is too dark to see.

If more than one candle is being used, others should now be lit in silence.

Meditation
The light of Christ
is the love of God his Father.
For a few moments now let the words of God
'You are precious in my eyes and I love you'
echo within you as you look at the candle.

I love you, says God.
Do you believe him?
Really believe him, take him at his word,
that he loves you,
all of you.
Love and light
is accepting you fully
forgiving you fully
calling you into his life
as you now turn to him
and allow love,
as sure as this candle-flame,
burn gently and warmly within you.

Pause, with or without music, for meditation and thought

Final Prayer
May the light of Christ be bright and warm in your life,
may it touch selfishness and sin and light you with forgiveness;
may it be encouraging and may it be the light of friendship;
may love touch others from you as the candle now touches your heart.
May you be filled with the love of the Father, the friendship of Jesus and the forgiveness of the Holy Spirit.

As people leave the room or chapel, they put their hands over the candle and make a silent prayer, allowing the candle to touch them with its flame and light before they go forth among people again.

18. Christmas

Setting of the place of prayer might include some signs of Christmas – a crib, a tree, with some symbolic reminders of poverty and of neglect. The prayer should begin with the placing of these symbols to the accompaniment of some Christmas music, played or sung. The crib might be introduced last with the following prayer, as one of the group place a candle in front of it:

Lord Jesus, light of the world,
Mary, light of God's people,
Joseph light of holiness,
pray with us now to God our Father.
Lord Jesus, come to birth in each of us,
as we live our lives like you;
come to birth in our society
as we try to treat each other
as brothers and sisters in God our Father.

Meditation

The joy and mystery of Christmas is well-expressed in this poem:

In this night
the stars left their habitual places
and kindled wildfire tidings
that spread faster than sound
In this night
the shepherds left their posts
to shout the new slogans
into each other's clogged ears
In this night
the foxes left their warm burrows
and the lion spoke with deliberation
'this is the end
revolution'
In this night
roses fooled the earth
and began to bloom
in the snow.

Dorothy Soelle, *Revolutionary Patience.*

Gospel Lk 7:18-23 and Lk 2:15-20

We look now at two gospel incidents – the first of the ministry of Jesus when he showed his care and concern for people. That was why he came: 'that we might have life to the full,' the life of brotherhood and friendship. Then we listen to some of the simple story of his birth. May he come to birth again in our world as he comes to birth through us.

A reading from the holy Gospel according to Luke

1. The disciples of John gave him all this news, and John, summoning two of his disciples, sent them to the Lord to ask, 'Are you the one who is to come, or must we wait for someone else?' When the men reached Jesus they said, 'John the Baptist has sent us to you, to ask, "Are you the one who is to come or have we to wait for someone else?"' It was just then that he cured many people of diseases and afflictions and of evil spirits, and gave the gift of sight to many who were blind. Then he gave the messengers their answer, 'Go back and tell John what you have seen and heard: the blind see again, the lame walk, lepers are cleansed, and the deaf hear, the dead are raised to life, the Good News is proclaimed to the poor and happy is the man who does not lose faith in me.'

2. Now when the angels had gone from them into heaven, the shepherds said to one another, 'Let us go to Bethlehem and see this thing that has happened which the Lord has made known to us.' So they hurried away and found Mary and Joseph, and the baby lying in the manger. When they saw the child they repeated what they had been told about him, and everyone who heard it was astonished at what the shepherds had to say. As for Mary, she treasured all these things and pondered them in her heart. And the shepherds went back glorifying and praising God for all they had heard and seen; it was exactly as they had been told.

This is the Gospel of the Lord.

Some faith-sharing might follow. Anyone who wishes might like to say how the Gospel stories just read struck them. . . what the Gospel would say to him/her about Christmas. . . and then might like to give some answer to the question: 'How will you bring the message of Christ to birth yourself this Christmas?'

Christmas Meditation

Each paragraph might be read by a different person:

Nobody expected him just like that: a baby, a manger, a young man, a young woman.
Nobody expected that his first visitors would be shepherds,
Little thought of in the eyes of the great.
Yes, he has come, but not as we expected.

The kings of the time had sons and daughters, but who remembers them now?
Who would know now of Herod, except that He had spoken of him?
Who would have thought that more people in today's world know of Nazareth
a poverty-stricken, sleepy townland,
than know of Antioch or Alexandria,
the places big in the minds and on the tongues of the time,
but not big in the heart of God?

Our notions of fame and success are turned upside-down.
Long after Herod's castles have turned to ruin, the cave of Bethlehem stands strong and holy,
a place of hope for generations yet unborn
because one starry night the Son of God was born there.
Only the heart that wants to love and love forever can recognise the beauty of God in the darkness of the cave.
Only such hearts can see greatness and dignity in the shepherd.
Only such hearts can see in this child the glory and life of God.

We didn't expect that later he would walk our bloodstained earth and share the sweat of our toil and agony and sadness, as he still walks this day.
Nor that he would laugh with the happy just because they were happy.
Nor that he would be nailed to a wooden cross so that the life of man would mingle with the blood of man's death
and the love of God displayed in Jesus, would conquer.

Nor did we expect that he would say things like
'He who sees you sees me'
or 'What you do for the least of my people you do for me.'

It's strange and unexpected that God would reach out to touch mankind
through the hands of an infant in a poor farmyard.
And it's strange, though beautiful, that our song,
Glory to God and peace on earth,
is a call to be his peace, justice and his music on earth.

Can we honestly sing 'Come, all ye faithful'
when what God means is
'Come to my Bethlehem,
and my Bethlehem is no longer a hillside cave
but it is where you create friendship, justice and love
among each other and bring Christ my son to birth?'

After a short pause play some Christmas music, or, if possible, the group sings a Christmas hymn.

Prayer for Others

This prayer is to remember in intercession people we want to pray for at Christmas. Simply call out the intentions. The first few are given here. Invite the group to make their own after these.

RESPONSE Lord Jesus, hear our prayer.
For each of our families. ℟.
For those who are lonely at Christmas. ℟.
For ourselves that we are aware of others' poverty and sadness
at Christmas. ℟.
That everyone here has a happy Christmas. ℟.
For people in prison. ℟.
For people away from home. ℟.

Final Prayer

Come, Lord Jesus, into our world
of love and work,
of pain and joy,
of hope and doubt.
Come with your gift of joy and peace
this Christmas,
to us and all we meet.
Come to birth within us
and among us,
you, the Saviour of the world.

19. Prayer with Water

A bowl of water may be placed in the middle of the group, or at the top of the room/chapel where it can be easily seen. A candle can be lit beside it. While this is being done, some Scripture may be read by one or more of the group:

If only you knew what God is offering
and who it is that is saying to you:
Give me a drink,
you would have been the one to ask
and he would have given you living water.

Unless a man is born of water and the holy Spirit,
he cannot enter the kingdom of God.

Leader: This is the water of baptism, of growth in Christ, of forgiveness. It is a sign that we belong to God, that we are sons and daughters of God in Christ.
Let us approach now and sign ourselves with this water.

Prayer
Water – a sign of baptism, a sign of forgiveness, refreshment and renewal, life, growth and healing. Allow this symbol to lead you now to prayer:

Lord Jesus, you have invited us to new birth in the Spirit and in water: forgive sin in our lives, and let the water of your life be the forgiveness of our meanness and intolerance, our selfishness and greed.

Lord Jesus, your life is a constant call to refreshment and renewal; let us be renewed in your love, aware of your love for each of us, a love that is as sure and certain as the flow of the water of life.

Lord, as water grows our fruit and land, may each of us grow in love of you as we grow older, and grow in understanding, tolerance and justice in our lives.

Lord Jesus, healer of all who come to you, heal our divisions and our bitterness in the water of baptism and in the living water which you promise to us; may your love heal the wounds of our sins and the harshness of others in our lives.

Meditation
If only we could allow the good in us flow to others.
We fear to be honest
and we fear to be different.
We are threatened by the differences between us
instead of being enriched by them.
We are locked in by intolerance and by greed
so that we cannot touch each other's lives in hope and joy.
But we can, in the power of Jesus Christ.
The water of baptism is for everyone;
in this gift of God's love we are all equal;
not all the same, but equal in our dignity
as children of God, brothers and sisters to each other.

To each other now we offer peace
and we offer prayer.
As a sign of peace we offer the water of baptism
to each person here,
promise of God's love and friendship
made visible in the friendship of Jesus
and in the community of his people.

Each person now makes the sign of the cross on the person beside him/her with the water.

Final Prayer
Bless us, Lord, before we go;
may we be people who spread in our world
the peace of Jesus Christ,
the justice of his Gospel
and the love of his Father.
You are one God forever and ever.